Managerial Forensics

Managerial Forensics

J. Mark Munoz and Diana Heeb Bivona

Managerial Forensics

First published in 2016 by
Business Expert Press, LLC
222 East 46th Street, New York, NY 10017
www.businessexpertpress.com

ISBN-13: 978-1-63157-254-8 (paperback)
ISBN-13: 978-1-63157-255-5 (e-book)

Business Expert Press Corporate Governance Collection

Collection ISSN: 1948-0470 (print)
Collection ISSN: 1948-0415 (electronic)

Cover and interior design by Exeter Premedia Services Private Ltd., Chennai, India

First edition: 2016

10 9 8 7 6 5 4 3 2 1

Printed in the United States of America.

Abstract

Managerial forensics is the practice of gathering relevant corporate information for the purpose of analyzing and identifying reasons for managerial obstacles, mismanagement, bankruptcy, and corporate demise. This book assembles a cast of leading academic and business experts and shares their views on the best practices in corporate analysis. Following the notion that the past offers insights into the future, the book examines the maladies in contemporary business and offers strategies for corporate revival and turnaround.

Keywords

business analysis, business consulting, business strategy, business turnaround, management analysis, management strategy, management turnaround, managerial forensics, organizational analysis, organizational development

Contents

Acknowledgments...ix

About the Contributors xi

Part I   **Understanding Managerial Forensics** 1

Chapter 1   Introduction 3
J. Mark Munoz and Diana Heeb Bivona

Chapter 2   From Problem to Cause 11
Diana Heeb Bivona

Chapter 3   Featherston Resources: A New, Clean, Green Fertilizer
Business That Failed.......................................21
Sergio Biggemann and Alan Collier

Chapter 4   Trust and Legal Considerations in Managerial
Forensics..47
Zheng Liu and Alice de Jonge

Part II   **Tools in Managerial Forensics** 65

Chapter 5   Internal Governance Structures and Corporate
Behavior 67
Alice de Jonge

Chapter 6   Assessing Leadership Preparedness 87
Anthony Liberatore and J. Mark Munoz

Chapter 7   Developing Evidence Based Data on Ethics and
Culture 103
Duane Windsor

Chapter 8   How to Perform an Autopsy on Marketing Strategy......117
Donald E. Sexton

Chapter 9   Forensic Accounting: Show Me the Money 135
Scott P. McHone and Tricia-Ann Smith DaSilva

Chapter 10   Forensic Accounting for Governmental Entities 151
D. Larry Crumbley

Chapter 11   Entrepreneurial Forensics: Assessing Customers
             and Decision Makers in the Biomedical Field................177
             Michael S. Kinch and Emre Toker

Chapter 12   International Forensics 193
             J. Mark Munoz

Part III   Strategies for Corporate Revival 209

Chapter 13   Executive Interview on Managerial Forensics: Keith
             Cooper, Senior Managing Director, FTI Finance
             and FTI Consulting 211
             J. Mark Munoz

Chapter 14   Team Health: Measuring It, Understanding It, and
             Improving It...217
             Colin Price and Sharon Toye

Chapter 15   Protecting Value via Information Management 235
             Al Naqvi

Chapter 16   Changing Direction 251
             Diana Heeb Bivona

Part IV   Conclusion 261

Chapter 17   Conclusion..263
             J. Mark Munoz and Diana Heeb Bivona

Index 273

Acknowledgments

The editors wish to thank their families, friends, and colleagues for all the support during the creation of this book. The professionalism and innovativeness demonstrated by all contributing authors led to the timely completion of the book and the advancement of management thinking.

About the Contributors

Sergio Biggemann is a Senior Lecturer in Marketing at the University of Otago. His research focus is on the Dynamics of Business Relationships, the Creation and Implementation of Business Solutions. His current research project is on the effects of business solutions on the supplier's network position as a source of competitive advantage.

Alan Collier is an engineer, lawyer, and businessman who still practices in all three areas. He holds a PhD in business and has a keen interest in measuring the performance of companies. He has worked as a consultant, postgraduate student and academic coordinator at the University of Otago for some years. He has also founded and run start-up businesses.

D. Larry Crumbley is the KPMG Endowed Professor at the Louisiana State University. He is a contributor of nine articles to the *Accounting Review* (very few tax articles ever appear here), and at least seven articles in the *Journal of Accountancy*, six articles in the *Journal of Taxation*, three in *The Tax Adviser*, eleven in the *CPA Journal*, two in *The Journal of ATA*, fifteen in *Petroleum Accounting* and *Financial Mgt. J.*, seven in *Tax Notes*, and one in *Tax Law Review*, *National Tax Journal*, *Advances in Taxation*, *Advances in Accounting Education*, *Journal of Accounting*, *Organization, and Society*, and *Journal of Risk and Insurance*. He is the author or coauthor of at least 350 major articles and many newspaper columns and has been quoted or praised in *New York Times*, *Washington Post*, *U.S. News & World Report*, *Wall Street Journal*, *Tax Notes*, *Business Week*, *Fortune*, *Forbes*, *Houston Chronicle*, *Houston Post*, *Chronicle of Higher Education*, *The Big Eight Review*, *Accounting News*, *Philadelphia Inquirer*, *Baltimore Sun*, *Baltimore Business Journal*, Paul Harvey noon news show (2-28-89), and many other newspapers, radio and television stations.

Tricia-Ann Smith DaSilva, BsC, CA, CPA, CISA, CRISC, CrFA, MBA is a Senior Manager at PricewaterhouseCoopers Jamaica with over 11 years experience in providing IT, Internal, and financial audit services. She is also a Board Member of the American Board of Forensic Accounting and a Member of the local Chapter Formation Committee of Information Systems Audit and Control Association.

Diana Heeb Bivona is the owner of an international business and management consulting firm. Her focus is emerging and developing markets. Prior to starting her own business ten years ago, she worked in a variety of administrative and managerial roles in industries including executive recruiting, structured settlements, education, investigative services, and retail. Diana teaches entrepreneurship, international business, management, and organizational leadership courses at several area universities. She holds an MBA from New York Institute of Technology and is currently pursuing a Doctorate of Business specializing in International Business.

Alice de Jonge is a senior lecturer in law at Monash Business School, Australia, where she teaches and researches in Comparative Asian Law and International Law. She is the author of three books on corporate governance issues in an international context, as well as various book chapters and journal articles.

Michael S. Kinch, PhD is Associate Vice Chancellor at Washington University in St Louis, where he helps lead the creation of innovative opportunities to foster corporate-academic partnerships. Prior to joining Washington University in July, 2014, he was Managing Director of the Center for Molecular Discovery at Yale University, Chief Scientific Officer at Functional Genetics, Inc. in Gaithersburg, MD and head of the Departments of Cancer Biology and In Vivo Biology at MedImmune, Inc. He has published more than 100 manuscripts, been granted 15 U.S. patents, and published more than 100 pending patents.

Anthony Liberatore is Millikin University's Hermann Chair of Management Development and Director of The Tabor School of Business MBA program. Dr. Liberatore coauthored a widely distributed Quarterly Economic and Financial Forecast for over a decade and has been selected a number of times for the Tabor School Teaching Excellence Award. He has served as a senior government advisor, been a small business owner, served on a number of boards, and consulted with scores of companies around the country on business, management, and leadership development. Dr. Liberatore is currently the Chairman of the Board of Illini Corporation, an Illinois bank holding company.

Dr. Zheng Liu is a lecturer in the International Business School Suzhou, Xi'an Jiaotong-Liverpool University. She gained her PhD at the Institute for Manufacturing, University of Cambridge with the research topic "The Development of Inter-firm Trust in Different National Culture Contexts: cases from the animation game industry." Her current research interests include cross-culture management, supply chain and operations, and creative industry.

Dr. Scott P. McHone, CPA, PhD has been providing accounting solutions since 1986. Along with being a Certified Public Accountant, Scott is also a Certified Forensic Accountant and a Chartered Global Management Accountant, and has also earned a certificate in Six Sigma. Scott owns and operates a CPA firm in California and is also the Executive Director of the American Board of Forensic Accounting.

J. Mark Munoz is a Professor of International Business at Millikin University in Illinois, and a former Visiting Fellow at the Kennedy School of Government at Harvard University. He is a recipient of several awards including three Best Research Paper Awards, a literary award, an international book award, and the ACBSP Teaching Excellence Award among others. Aside from top-tier journal publications, he has authored and edited and coedited nine books namely: *Land of My Birth, Winning Across Borders, In Transition, A Salesman in Asia, Handbook of Business Plan Creation, International Social Entrepreneurship, Contemporary Micro-enterprises: Concepts and Cases, Handbook on the Geopolitics of Business* and *Hispanic-Latino Entrepreneurship.* As Chairman and CEO of international management consulting firm Munoz and Associates International, he directs consulting projects worldwide in the areas of strategy formulation, business development, and international finance.

Al Naqvi is the System CFO and EVP of Illinois Health and Science, the parent company of Decatur Memorial Hospital. He has multidisciplinary background in behavioral finance, information technology, and investment management. Prior to joining IHS, he worked in financial services, strategy consulting, investment banking, and information technology. He also served as the VP of AES, a Fortune 500 energy company; and in the accounting and finance organization of Nabisco Foods group. His former company was a leader in strategy and financial services consulting and investment banking for the Nuclear Medicine industry. Mr. Naqvi has designed and conceptualized over 100 use cases for big data—including several for Fannie Mae, the world's largest financial services company. He has written several articles on Big Data and has presented in big data conferences. His current focus is on Big Data for Healthcare industry. He holds an MBA from New York Institute of Technology and has an Executive Certificate from UVA, Darden School of Business.

Colin Price is Chairman of Co Company, a boutique consulting firm focused on organizational health. For many years the worldwide leader of McKinsey's Organisation Practice. Author of seven books and speaker at major events. Visiting professor at Said School of Management at Oxford University.

Donald E. Sexton Professor of Marketing and Decisions, Risk, and Operations, Columbia University, has been teaching for more than forty-five years at Columbia and is a recipient of the Business School's Distinguished Teaching Award. Don has taught at several institutions including the University of California-Berkeley, INSEAD, and the China Europe International Business School and his numerous articles have appeared in journals such as the *Harvard Business Review, Journal of Marketing Research,* and *Management Science.* His best-selling books, *Marketing 101* and *Branding 101,* have been translated into several languages including Chinese, Russian, Turkish, and Indonesian and his most recent book, *Value Above Cost,* explains how marketing determines financial performance and is available in Chinese. Don received the Marketing Trends Award for his work on marketing and branding strategy and is President of the New York American Marketing Association.

Emre Toker has extensive experience as a scientist, an entrepreneur, an innovation and entrepreneurship mentor, and an active angel investor and is the Managing Director of the Skandalaris Center for Interdisciplinary Innovation and Entrepreneurship at Washington University in St. Louis. After studying Physics at Reed College and Electrical Engineering at the California Institute of Technology and the University of Arizona, Mr. Toker founded two biomedical technology companies in Tucson, MedOptics and Bioptics Corporations, and cofounded one in Santa Clara, California, Radicon Imaging Corporation, each acquired within seven years of founding.

CHAPTER 1

Introduction

J. Mark Munoz and Diana Heeb Bivona

The idea for managerial forensics sprung from a recent curriculum redesign effort in a business school at a private university in the U.S. Midwest. As educators, an emphasis needed to be placed on ensuring that the curriculum prepared students for whatever business endeavors they elected to pursue after graduating. As a performance-based institution, teaching students practical, hands-on, relevant techniques and applications was the school's hallmark. Therefore, with each course, the standard question is, "What tools do we want students to have?"

The authors envisioned a course that would serve as a critical thinking performance lab of sorts for understanding the complexity of business failures. This course would provide students with an opportunity to further develop critical thinking skills, understand the cross-disciplinary nature of business problems, and practice techniques and strategies pivotal to identifying and diagnosing problematic business issues. Thus, the seeds for managerial forensics were planted and a discussion for creation of a practical framework and model that would aid business managers confronting the prospect of business failure sprouted.

The Diverse Path to Failure

The contemporary business environment is extremely challenging. It forces organizations to be nimble, aggressive, intuitive, innovative, and highly efficient. It has created a new breed of managers who think outside the box and operate in nonconventional ways. It has led to a new culture of business and contributed to the evolution of the new corporate reality of the 21st century.

Not all companies successfully adapt and reinvent themselves to meet the demands of contemporary business. A large number of businesses go bankrupt each year as illustrated by a U.S. Court's report, which indicated that 1,000,083 bankruptcies had been filed in the 12-month period ending June 30, 2014.[1]

There are diverse reasons that led to these bankruptcies. Moya K Mason Research identified 11 common causes of business failure: choosing a nonprofitable business, lack of cash reserve, failure to define market, poor pricing, lack of cash flow planning, poor competitive planning, overgeneralization, overdependence on one customer, uncontrolled growth, overestimated capabilities, and inadequate management.[2] They are not the only ones to attempt to identify a common set of causes. Probst and Raisch categorized the typical causes of failure as the premature aging syndrome (i.e., slow growth, unclear change, poor leadership, without a success-driven culture) and the burnout syndrome (i.e., extensive growth, unmanaged change, overly dominant leadership, and with an excessively success-driven culture).[3]

Researchers continue in their quest to find a specific, uniform set of criteria that conclusively identify why business fail, but one has yet to materialize. There are common themes though that run through many business failure theories, and one such dominant theme is that the leading causes of business failure are largely a result of courses of action taken by an organization and its management. Following this notion, the authors believe that this is the area where managerial forensics offers real value and a pathway for business revival and transformation.

Defining the Managerial Forensic Approach

Managerial forensics is an approach to diagnosing, framing, and solving problems. It is the practice of gathering historical corporate data for the

---

[1] U.S. Courts. 2014. http://www.uscourts.gov/uscourts/Statistics/Bankruptcy Statistics/BankruptcyFilings/2014/0614_f2.pdf (accessed October 16, 2014).

[2] MKM Research. 2014. http://www.moyak.com/papers/small-business-failure.html (accessed October 16, 2014).

[3] Probst, G., and S. Raisch. 2005. "Organizational Crisis: The Logic of Failure." *Academy of Management Executive* 19, no. 1, pp. 90–105.

purpose of analyzing and identifying reasons for management obstacles, mismanagement, bankruptcy, and corporate demise. Managerial forensics seeks to effectively marry the best of two disciplines: management and science. Management holds the reigns of leadership and is ultimately responsible for the health and well-being of an organization. The primary purpose of science is to explain and predict in a systematic and methodical manner.

Managers handle multiple areas of responsibility ranging from planning, organizing, and staffing to leading, controlling, and motivating. In times of crisis, they are the helmsmen. They are the ones we believe the managerial forensics approach will benefit the most.

When a business fails, management often takes the blame, with *poor management* cited repeatedly as the culprit. Hindsight suggests that those many failures are avoidable, and that management should have recognized the red flags. This begs the question, "Why didn't they?" Most business failures do not occur overnight. They fester and build over time; so, how could management not see what was coming?

One could speculate that they were in denial or simply inept. However, what if they failed to correctly diagnose the problem because they failed to utilize the correct data, analysis, and tools? What if they were too close, too involved, overtly dependent on their gut instinct, or adamant that a "fix" worked so well before that it would again? Or could prior success have led a manager to ignore other relevant business factors in carrying out a decision?[4]

Could a framework be created to overcome many of these issues and set an organization, poised on the brink of failure, on a course of recovery? Could decisions be made based on rigorous logic and a detailed analysis of the totality of facts? The authors believed so and turned to the tenants of science as a means of ensuring that decisions, when made, were based on the totality of facts and not gut instincts or superficial analysis.

Why science? Science is grounded in the methodical and the systematic. The exploratory process of scientific inquiry provides a means by which

---

[4] Audia, P.G., E.A. Locke, and K.G. Smith. 2000. "The Paradox of Success: An Archival and a Laboratory Study of Strategic Persistence Following a Radical Environmental Change." *Academy of Management Journal* 43, pp. 837–53.

managers can ask questions and dig for answers. It is a method that encourages a thorough investigation using a set of relevant tools to gather, analyze, and interpret data. A rigorous approach that when followed leads to new insights and solutions. Such an approach would benefit managers faced with an impending failure, and offer a foundational framework and set of tools that support the managerial forensics approach.

Even when faced with a challenging business landscape, the authors believe that many companies can potentially be saved, if proper management analysis and the right set of tools are introduced that can help resuscitate a company suffering from stagnation or decline. Understanding the root causes of business failures through a scientific lens can help managers identify viable solutions backed by evidence. Additionally, by studying the failures of other firms, decision makers begin to question their knowledge and think differently.[5]

Keller and Price highlighted the need to examine nine elements of organizational health—direction, leadership, culture and climate, accountability, coordination and control, capabilities, motivation, external orientation, and innovation and learning.[6] These are the areas that require close examination. It is here where the authors see the greatest opportunity to create management tools that will aid not only in preventing corporate demise, but in breathing new life into a failing business.

Driven by this need to develop a scientific approach and create management tools that can resuscitate ailing companies and contribute to corporate vigor, the authors embarked on a global quest to identify and gather the best practices in organizational analysis and management.

On this journey of discovery, it quickly became evident that a common cause of business failure was the subjectivity of decision making rather than much needed objectivity. In essence, when management is treated more as an extension of a manager's individual style rather than an exact science grounded in facts and analysis, the propensity for bad

---

[5] Baum, J.A., and K.B. Dahlin. 2007. "Aspiration Performance and Railroads' Patterns of Learning from Train Wrecks and Crashes." *Organization Science* 18, pp. 368–85.

[6] Keller, S., and C. Price. September 2011. "What Matters Most." *Financial Executive*, 30–33.

judgments is higher. Individuals ultimately act from their perceived reality as opposed to an objective reality, and this perception gap leads to significant managerial problems.[7] It is why the authors support the position that evidence-based, scientifically grounded approaches like managerial forensics heighten the probability of operational success and corporate restructuring.

Quest for the Tools of Managerial Forensics

In this book, the authors expand the understanding of managerial forensics, offer tools for its corporate application, and identify strategies for corporate turnarounds and revival. The book is organized into three sections and covers these three topics. In the concluding chapter, findings and conclusions are presented and the equivalent of a "surgical tool kit" for managerial forensics is presented.

The book is divided into four sections. Part I defines the pioneering approach of managerial forensics and the existing research on the causes of organizational failure. Part II introduces a compilation of insights and experiences from leading business professionals and academics around the world who support the organizational-approach managerial forensics advocates. These chapters offer specific examples and tools that managers and consultants can use in analyzing organizational malaise or morbidity. Part III focuses on ways managerial forensics can be used to restore organizational health and contribute to business turnarounds. Part IV contains the authors' concluding thoughts.

Part I: Understanding Managerial Forensics

- Introduction (*J. Mark Munoz and Diana Heeb Bivona*)
- From Problem to Cause (*Diana Heeb Bivona*)

---

[7] Ferris, G.R., G. Adams, R.W. Kolodinsky, W.A. Hochwarter, and A.P. Ammeter. 2002. "Perceptions of Organizational Politics: Theory and Research Directions." In *Research in Multi-level Issues Volume 1: The Many Faces of Multi-Level Issues*, eds. F.J. Yammarino and F. Dansereau, 179–254. Kidlington, OX: Elsevier Science.

of symptoms in a diagnosis. Students are told "when you hear hoof beats, look for horses, not zebras" meaning look for the simplest explanation first.

For example, if a patient presents to a physician with a runny nose, chills, and fever, it is likely that it is flu and not malaria. Thus, by examining and performing a simple test for the flu first saves valuable resources trying to rule out a diagnosis of malaria. The same approach can be applied in business by remembering to examine analytically the most logical and simplest explanation first before delving into the more complex one.

In situations where the primary cause is not visible or readily known, a deeper analysis of systems and processes is needed. A thorough review of these business components may expose several issues that merge into a pattern that may point the way to the identification of a specific cause. Another more specific reason may also emerge during the evaluation.

In medicine, physicians use a mnemonic based on etiology to ensure that a thorough, systematic, and organized differential of a patient occurs. The mnemonic used in medicine is VINDICATES:

- V—Vascular
- I—Inflammatory
- N—Neoplastic
- D—Degenerative or Deficiency
- I—Idiopathic, Intoxication
- C—Congenital
- A—Autoimmune or Allergic
- T—Traumatic
- E—Endocrine
- S—Psychosocial or Something else

We propose the adoption of a similarly styled mnemonic to ensure a thorough and systematic review of business systems in identifying potential causes. That mnemonic is SOAP. A fitting analogy as we view this process of eliminating problems as a *cleansing*:

- S—Sales and marketing
- O—Organizational structure and leadership